D0956036

ZEN

THE REASON OF UNREASON

EASTERN WISDOM

CHRONICLE BOOKS
SAN FRANCISCO

A Labyrinth Book

First published in the United States in 1993 by Chronicle Books.

Copyright © 1993 by Labyrinth Publishing (UK) Ltd.

Design by Meringue Management

The Little Wisdom Library–Eastern Wisdom was produced by Labyrinth Publishing (UK) Ltd. Printed and bound in Singapore by Craft Print Pte. Ltd.

Library of Congress Cataloging in Publication Data: Zen, Eastern Wisdom.

p. cm. (Eastern Wisdom) Includes bibliographical references.

ISBN 0–8118–0403–8:

1. Zen Buddhism. I. Chronicle Books (Firm) II. Series.

BQ9265.6.Z45 1993

294. 3'927– – dc20   92–42257

CIP

Distributed in Canada by Raincoast Books,

112 East Third Avenue, Vancouver, B.C. V5T 1C8

10 9 8 7 6 5 4 3 2 1

Chronicle Books

275 Fifth Street, San Francisco, CA 94103

Introduction

Zen Buddhism is already without a doubt the form of East Asian Buddhism best known in the West, and with good reason. Zen teachings embody even today a deep, authentic seriousness of purpose, and a desire to dispense with all distractions of language and thought to concentrate on the ultimate goal of enlightenment. Through the centuries, this attraction to Zen may be traced back to a remarkable story of doubt and affirmation. Chinese Buddhists of the age that gave rise to Zen lived in a world in which the serene, untroubled spirituality we tend to associate with the East was conspicuously absent. The Buddha had, after all, lived far away, in another civilization. Trying to interpret his doctrines seemed to lead only to irreconcilable clashes between his latter-day devotees, a slide into formalism, and, it seemed, complete irreligion.

No wonder Bodhidharma, who had talked of direct access to the truth, gripped the imagination of serious thinkers. For was not meditation, on which he had concentrated, a skill passed on from master to disciple going back to

---

Previous page: A Zen monk sitting in sazen in the monastery courtyard. *Above:* Wax bowl decoration of Chinese characters

---

Buddha himself? Ultimately, Chinese masters took confidence from that spiritual lineage, for they realized that, for all the barriers of time and space, full enlightenment was to be found within.

An undeniable age of decline, however, burst upon them in a great rush of rebellion, invasion, and violent political infighting. If the "Golden Age of Zen," as recalled in the many anecdotes concerning the great eighth, ninth, and tenth century Chinese masters, seems one of harsh shouting and harsher beating, this is but a pale reflection of the chaos that often surrounded them: burning, looting, even cannibalism. Far from being irresponsible pranksters, the masters in such a world had to be committed to the utterly unflinching pursuit of truth.

In a gentler age, flowers and poetry may form an appropriate part of Zen's repertory—it has indeed been a civilizing influence, especially in medieval Japan. But that particular civilization could all so easily have been snuffed out, had not Zen monks provided the spiritual discipline that enabled Japan's rulers to face the terrifying threat of massive Mongol invasions. That Zen is not easily grasped or practiced the following pages will show. If it has proved attractive to Western inquirers, it is not because it merely soothes the itch for the exotic. At its core it is hard, diamond-hard.

T.H. Barrett
Professor of East Asian History
University of London

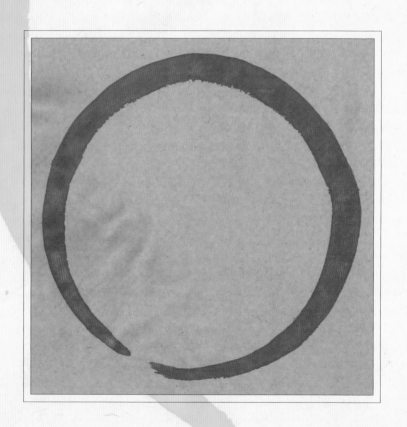

The Essence Of Zen

en is, in many ways, the simplest of phenomena, yet to explain it is perhaps the most difficult thing in the world. Zen is a kind of festivity, not a scholarship, for its very basis is not of the mind, not rational or defined; it does not take its essence from the cultured mind. It is never borrowed or derived from scriptures as are many religious beliefs or dogmas.

Zen is a living flower, a rose that lasts forever - beginningless and endless - with petals that fall while new petals grow, in a constant state of change. Yet at its center, Zen never changes.

We can begin our attempt at "explaining" Zen with a Zen story that derives from the great master Ma-tsu, known as Baso in Japan, who lived and worked in China between 709 and 788. The story is told in the form of a conversation between Ma-tsu and the Chinese scholar-monk Liang of Hsi-shan.

Ma-tsu asked Liang: "What sutra are you lecturing on?"

> **THE SOLITARY BIRD, CUCKOO OF THE FOREST**
>
> Kinzan, Ganto and Seppo were doing Zazen when Tozan came in with the tea.
>
> Kinzan shut his eyes. Tozan asked, "Where are you going?" Kinzan replied, "I am entering dhyana." Tozan said, "Dhyana has no gate; how can you enter into it?"

Right: The influence of Zen led the samurai culture of Japan to develop such refined arts as the tea ceremony and flower arranging.

"The mind sutra," Liang replied.

"By what do you lecture?" Ma-tsu asked.

"With mind."

Whereupon Ma-tsu said, "The mind is like an actor, the meaning like a jester, the six senses like an acquaintance; how can the mind lecture on a sutra?"

Liang answered, "If mind cannot lecture, can't no-mind?"

"Yes, no-mind can lecture all right."

At this point Liang began to leave, but Ma-tsu called to him and said, "Professor!" Liang turned back towards Ma-tsu, who said, "From birth to death, this is how it is."

Following this encounter Liang's whole body was drenched in sweat and on his way back to the temple he said to his monks:

"I thought it could be said that all my life, no one could lecture better than I on the sutras. Today, a question from Ma-tsu dissolved the ice of a lifetime."

After this Liang gave up his lectures and retired far into the mountains and was never heard from again.

The essential meaning of this story lies in the understanding that the mind cannot indicate the ultimate, cannot reveal the truth.

When Liang asks Ma-tsu, "If mind cannot lecture, can't no-mind?" this is a rational question, from

the mind. Logically, if the mind cannot lecture then the no-mind can. But Matsu's answer effectively thrust Liang into a state of no-mind: "Yes, no-mind can lecture all right. From birth to death this is how it is."

The Zen understanding, at its very essence, is that the mind is unreliable, it changes throughout life as it accumulates knowledge, opinions, and ideas, whereas no-mind is always the same; unpolluted, always singing the truth whether we hear it or not. Its dance is eternal.

"Soundless and without scent, heaven and earth are incessantly repeating unwritten sutras."

This is Zen. To get a further sense of the qualities of Zen, it is important to know its beginnings.

Left: The ancient ceremonial 'Tea-Master'. Here rendered in fine ivory and lacquer.
Above: Portable water container, used for the tea ceremony, decorated with a bamboo design.

Shakyamuni On The Mount Of The Holy Vulture

In the same way as the basic philosophy of Zen is somehow "intentionally" or intrinsically hard to grasp as a logical concept, so also the beginnings of Zen are clouded in mystery and legend. Although Zen itself has its origins in China, where Zen monasteries were first established, its fundamental roots reach to the native soil of Buddhism in India. It is also important to remember, however, that Zen and Buddhism are not one and the same. There are many forms of Buddhism other than Zen forms. Zen legend grew from the presence of Buddha himself, indeed, from a very beautiful story. According to legend, the birth of the understanding that was to become Zen occurred as a single moment of great significance during a discourse held by the Buddha, then named Shakyamuni. The story is entirely appropriate to the deepest essence of truth, the power of no-mind, as it developed within Zen philosophy.

Shakyamuni was engaged at the Mount of the Holy Vulture in preaching to a

> A monk asked Ganto, "When the Three Worlds are attacking us, what shall we do?"
>
> "Sit still!" said Ganto. The monk was surprised and said, "Please explain a little more."
>
> "Bring me Mount Ro," said Ganto, "and I will tell you."

Previous page: A statue of the Buddha sitting in the lotus pose inspires the inhabitants of a Zen monastery. Right: A finely decorated *shakudo-nanakoji tsuba*, the hilt of a Zen sword.

gathering of his disciples. He sat upon the podium completely silent for a long time, and instead of resorting to any lengthy discourse to explain his point that day, he lifted a single lotus flower and held it in his hand for all to see. No one understood the meaning of his gesture except the venerable Mahakashyapa, who quietly smiled at Shakyamuni, as if he fully comprehended the meaning of this silent teaching. Shakyamuni, perceiving the smile, declared, "I have the most precious treasure, spiritual and transcendental, which this moment I hand over to you, O venerable Mahakashyapa!"

Zen followers generally agree that this incident is the origin of their doctrine, for by raising the flower Shakyamuni symbolically revealed the innermost mind of the Buddha. The spirit of

Zen is conveyed in what happened to Mahakashyapa, who, by letting the silence of the master penetrate the very core of his being, understood its deep significance. The master is silent, the disciple smiles, the two minds are one.

Zen has been called "the diamond thunderbolt" because it is a sudden experience. Suddenly Mahakashyapa opened his eyes and saw the lotus flower held by his master; suddenly it was as though a thunderbolt had hit him and the sleep of millions of years was broken. In that awakening, he knew the mystery of existence and thus Shakyamuni gave to him his most precious treasure.

Like the conversation between Ma-tsu and Liang, this story tells us that Zen grew out of Buddha, not Buddhism, for Mahakashyapa then took his new awakening and made for the world what eventually became known as Zen.

Previous page: The sandals of Zen monks hang outside the monastery. *Above:* The hilt of a Zen sword. *Right:* A Zen monastery.

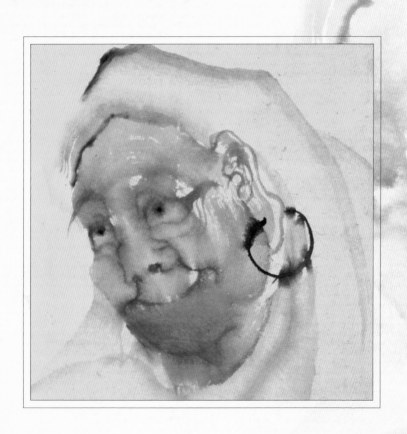

= =

Bodhidharma

t was a long time after that single, very significant event that Zen began to establish itself as a new mode of perceiving reality and the self. In the Zen school, Shakyamuni ranks as the first patriarch, Mahakashyapa as the second, followed by a line of twenty-eight Indian patriarchs, concluding with Bodhidharma. These masters all carried the original essence born out of Buddha's insight until it made its way into China.

Bodhidharma is said to have arrived in China from India in 520 A.D. He came to China with a special message, which is stated in the following lines:

"A fallen leaf returning to the branch? Butterfly."

"A special transmission outside the scriptures;
No dependence upon words and letters; - Direct pointing at the soul of man; - Seeing into one's nature and the attainment of Buddhahood."

Bodhidharma was a Buddhist monk who wandered into China carrying with him the essence of *dhyana* (Sanskrit for meditation) as taught by the Buddha. The historical records of his coming have been lost, but it is likely that Buddhist monks were being persecuted in India because their religion severely threatened the established Hindu code of behavior and class divisions, and, as such, were forced to seek refuge in Chinese monasteries.

Previous page: Bodhidharma, the last Indian patriarch who brought Zen into China from India. *Right:* A teapot, the quintessential symbol of the Zen tea ceremony. *Following page:* A portrait of Bodhidharma.

It is said that Bodhidharma stayed in the Shao-lin monastery in China, where he sat cross-legged staring at a blank wall for nine years, stating that he would not turn from the wall until someone of worth came to him. One day a monk called Shen-kuang visited him and implored Bodhidharma to enlighten him into the truth of *dhyana*. Bodhidharma paid no attention; but Shen-kuang persisted, for he knew that all the great spiritual leaders of the past had undertaken many a heart-rending trial in order to attain the final object of their aspiration. One evening he stood in the falling snow waiting for Bodhidharma to notice him, until at last the snow buried him to his knees. Finally, the master turned back and asked Shen-kuang what he wished him to do. The hopeful disciple replied that he wanted to receive instruction. Bodhidharma replied that the doctrine of the Buddha could only be understood through long and hard discipline and that there was nothing he could do. Exasperated by the master, Shen-kuang cut off his left arm with the sword he was carrying and presented it to Bodhidharma as a token of his sincerity in the desire to be instructed by him. The master at last condescended and told him to change his name to Hui-k'e.

According to the continuing legend, Bodhidharma instructed Chinese monks in the arts of the Buddha's teaching for a further nine years, at the end of which he announced that he wished to return to his native country, and that he wanted to know what their attainments were.

"Nine years had passed and he (Bodhidharma) now wished to return westward to India. He called his disciples and said: "The time has now come. Why does not each of you say what you have attained?"

The disciple Tao-fu replied: "As I see it, (the truth) neither adheres to words or letters nor is it separate from them. Yet it functions as the Way."

The Master said: You have attained my skin."

Then a nun, Tsung-chih, spoke: "As I understand it, (the truth) is like the auspicious glimpse of the Buddha land of Aksobhya; it is seen once, but not a second time."

The master replied: "You have attained my flesh." Tao-yu said: "The four great elements are originally empty; the five skandhas (aggregates) have no existence. According to my belief, there is no Dharma to be grasped."

To him the Master replied: "You have attained my bones."

Finally, there was Hui-k'e. He bowed respectfully and stood silent.

The Master said: You have attained my marrow."

Thus, the same essential qualities of Zen were born in China and became known as *Ch'an* from the Sanskrit *dhyana*, meaning "meditation."

From Dhyana To Ch'an To Zen

In the Zen school that eventually developed, one of the most important lessons, or koans, given from master to disciple was the question of why Bodhidharma had come from the West, and specifically from India. The answer lies in the fact that Bodhidharma brought with him the understanding of the experience of sudden enlightenment (Shakyamuni's and Mahakashyapa's enlightenment). This enlightenment was to be felt by many of the subsequent Zen disciples, some of whose stories are related here.

"One day Kyozan was looking at the moon together with Sekishitsu and asked him, "Where does the roundness of the moon go when it becomes sharp, crescent?" Sekishitsu said, "When it is sharp, the roundness is still there."

An abbess practicing Zen speaks to her disciples during their meditations: "How is it with nothingness?"
"I don't know," replies a young man who had been able to endure the difficulties of Zen practice only with great effort.
"How is it with nothingness?" the abbess asked again, hitting him on the legs with a stick.
At the moment he is struck, an exclamation of enlightenment bursts from the disciple's mouth: "Suddenly I feel that it has become bright. Oh, it is nothingness, this is nothingness, and that is nothingness."

Page 32: A fine foliate-shaped box decorated in gold depicts the nine-tailed fox disguised as the Chinese princess Dakki.
Right: Decorated hilt of a sword used in kendō.

Bodhidharma also brought the notion of the transmission of enlightenment from master, Shakyamuni, to disciple, Mahakashyapa, as well as a new way of meditation called *pi-kuan* in Chinese which consisted of sitting staring at a blank wall. These two essences of the deepest levels of the truth and practice of Zen are still with us today.

It was these teachings that evolved in India, traveled to China, and then to Japan, changing in name only from dhyana, to Ch'an, to Zen.

In Japan, at the time of the arrival of Zen, Buddhism was already deeply influencing the religious climate. When *Ch'an* monks and masters traveled to Japan from China they found a fertile soil for the new teachings; and with the coming of the teachings of the new understanding of enlightenment through Zen techniques, the whole of Buddha's original teaching became firmly established.

History tells us that the first master, considered the founder of Zen in Japan, was Eisai (1141-1215) who established its first school of learning. The word Zen was actually the Japanese pronunciation of *Ch'an*, or meditation. It was in Japan that Zen truly came to fruition and where the particular form of meditation, sitting in meditation, *tso-ch'an* in Chinese, and known as *zazen* in Japanese, became deeply embedded within the culture and religious structure of the country.

Here, Zen was also applied to a number of ways and arts that are today practiced throughout the world. Among these arts and disciplines are: the Zen way, *dō*; the Zen way of flowers, *kadō*; the Zen tea ceremony, *sadō*; the Zen way of the sword, *kendō*; of archery, *kyūdō*; and self-defense, *jūdō*; the Zen way of poetry, *kadō*; and of calligraphy, *shodō*. All are inspired by the spirit of Zen and performed in a meditative way.

Above: The tranquillity of a Zen garden. Zen monks work in the garden as a way of meditation.

Z e n –

T h a t W h i c h I s N o t

monk said to Ummon, *"What is your age, may I ask?"*
Ummon replied, "Seven times nine - sixty-eight."
The monk said, "What do you mean, 'Seven times nine - sixty-eight?'"
Ummon said, "I took off five years for your sake."

Zen is a specific state of awareness in which the mystery and beauty of life in the present is perceived wholly and directly, and in pure objectivity. Zen is foremost an experience, a sudden realization of what is, and as such it is stripped of all the elements which we normally associate with a religion. Alan Watts, the American theologian and philosopher, describes Zen:

"Zen is a way and a view of life which does not belong to any of the formal categories of modern Western thought. It is not a religion or a philosophy; it is not a psychology nor a type of science. It is an example of what in India is known as a 'way of liberation,' and is similar in this respect to Yoga, Taoism, and Vedanta. A way of liberation can have no positive definition." Rather, it is defined by that which is not, almost as though one was to find the essence of emptiness by peeling off the several skins of an onion."

Zen is a religious path with no theology. It exists and thrives through everyday conversation and advice given by the masters to their disciples in monasteries and schools. It is action according to reality—to what is.

Right: A circular dish portraying a master and his attendant.

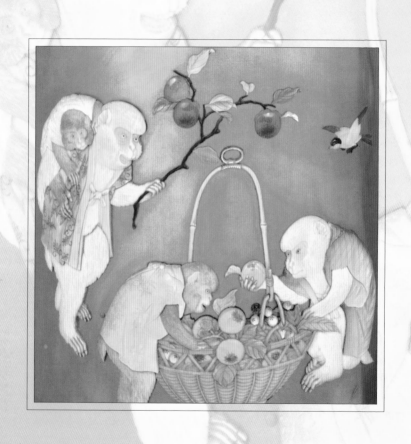

═

Zen Practice
Zazen And Satori

═

The training by which the modern pupil of Zen is enabled to relinquish his hold on his conceptual world is applied through four main avenues: zazen, sitting in meditation; koans, problems beyond logic; sanzen, private interviews with the master; and ordinary physical work in the monastery or its gardens, which brings the pupil in contact with everyday life.

Zen philosophy does not suggest that any method can awaken the mind to reality, since this implies a conscious effort to grasp something which simply is and is already present. However, the technique of zazen has emerged throughout the centuries since Zen began, and is considered a successful

Above: Hui Neng, the Sixth Patriarch of Zen, known for his uncompromising preference for firsthand experience.
Right: Zen kendō sword fittings.

and necessary tool to still the mind, allowing it to be relaxed and yet attentive, free and yet concentrated.

In zazen, the pupils sit cross-legged in the lotus position in a quiet room and by slow and rhythmic breathing bring the mind to a quiet state, free from tension and chatter. In some meditations, the pupil simply continues in this mode of being and allows thoughts to come and go as though they were clouds crossing the sky, neither holding on to them nor pushing them away. At other times, the pupil may meditate upon a koan set for him by the master, allowing it to drop into the mind like a stone thrown into a still pool. Sitting in zazen the pupil contemplates his or her own Buddha-nature. By casting off body and mind in the rigors of this discipline, one may realize enlightenment.

For the Zen disciple, practice inevitably brings enlightenment, perhaps through satori, the most dramatic of all Zen forms. Like all

mystical experiences, Zen satori is ineffable and cannot be satisfactorily described in words. Yet it is the central pivot of Zen; that which all its pupils aim to realize. In the breakthrough of the mind, achieved either by sitting in zazen or by contemplating a koan, or both, the universal unity of reality which encompasses the self and the cosmos is experienced.

The experience might be triggered by a sound heard while deep in meditation; the sound of the monastery's evening bell, the strokes of a clock, or the rain pattering on the ground. The liberating experience can also occur in the presence of the master who shocks the pupil, perhaps by a blow from his Zen stick or through some original and irrational statement. Opening the way to nothingness, such a shock sends the pupil to the ultimate realization.

Zen Flowers
Haikus And Koans

Haikus and koans are the quintessential expressions of Zen - the flowers that Zen masters have created for us through their wisdom.

The haiku contains few words. It exists as a brief and existential piece of writing intended to be visualized, and to cause the disciple, through its beauty, to fall into a deep, undisturbed peacefulness - into a state of meditation.

Silence is not just a word; the reader is lost in it. The high flight of the mandarin ducks leaves traces upon the eternal snow of the mountains.

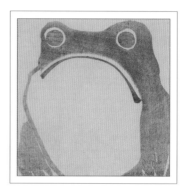

"Such silence;
snow-tracing wings
of mandarin ducks."

This page: The artful strokes of a brush immortalize the meditative quality of Zen paintings. *Next page, top right:* The gong is struck to call Zen monks to meditation. *Bottom left:* Moving from the center, like this spider in its web, Zen is mirrored in nature.

"Zen Master Seng-ts'an said,
The great Way is not difficult
if you don't cling to good
and bad.
Just let go of your preferences:
and everything will be perfectly
clear."

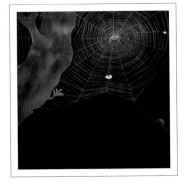

"Sitting silently
Doing nothing
Spring comes
And the grass grows by itself."

"Harvest Moon:
Around the pond I wander
And the night is gone."

Listen to each of these verses and remain silent in that moment. This is Zen. There is essentially nothing else. All judgments as to the value of haiku are ultimately fruitless, all attempts to use them as the basis for instruction or relevance are impotent, for the very essence of their existence is in their non-existence.

The exclusive existence of Zen within monastic life has always centered around the daily life of the master and his monks. This relationship became one of the sources from which the teachings were drawn. The exchanges and anecdotes between masters and disciples were used as koans, or means to aid the disciple inperceiving reality (enlightenment). The koan represents the fundamental essence of Zen teaching.

An anecdote or a question is given to the disciple who is to solve it by concen-

Above: Drawing patterns in the sand is a form of Zen meditation. *Right:* A figurine potraying a Japanese warrior. The whole structure of Japanese society was strongly influenced by the advent of Zen.

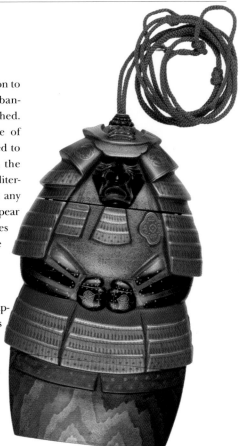

trating and devoting all his attention to it until all rational thinking is abandoned and enlightenment is reached. As Zen adheres to the doctrine of sudden enlightenment, as opposed to a gradual process of realization, the koans are constructed so that they literally force the pupil not to rely on any rational process. As such, koans appear paradoxical and sound like devices intended to drive the disciple "mad." They make no "sense" in the way that "rational" humanity is accustomed to.

"What is the sound of one hand clapping?" To the rational mind it is clearly impossible for one hand to clap, and even if it were possible, there would be no sound.

ZEN–THE REASON OF UNREASON

A monk had come to see Kuei-tsung and after a very brief stay was making his departure. Kuei-tsung said, "Where are you going?" The monk replied, "I'm going all over the place learning the five flavors of Zen." Kuei-tsung said, "Yes, there are the five flavors of Zen in various places, but here I have only one." The monk asked, "And what may be your one-flavored Zen?" Kuei-tsung struck him. The monk said, "I understand! I understand!" Kuei-tsung said, "Tell me what! Tell me what!" And as the monk began to speak, Kuei-tsung struck him again.

Kuei-tsung struck the monk to awaken him to that which is sleeping in us all. Zen cannot be expressed in words. The moment we start to explain it, we have missed it. We can be it, we can have it, and we can dance it, but we can never bring it into words, for then it is already absent. Zen is a wordless experience of our being.

A newcomer asked to be shown the way to the monastery, and Chao-chou replied: "Have you finished eating your rice? ... Then go wash your bowl!" Thereupon the monk gained instant enlightenment.

This is a perfect example of the most enigmatic of Zen koans. Chao-chou's statement seems to say nothing, but if we listen to the verse written by Wu-men corresponding to it, we gain some element of enlightenment:

"Since it is all too clear,
It takes time to grasp it.
When you understand that it's foolish to look for fire with fire,
The meal is already cooked."

Chao-chou's master, Nan-ch'uan, once killed a cat that was the object of discord amongst the monks. Hearing of his master's actions, Chao-chou put his sandals on his head. The great Zen writer and master D.T. Suzuki often used this device of placing his shoes on his head simply in order to demonstrate the obvious irrationality of Zen.

A monk came from Ting-chou's assembly to Wu-chiu, who said to him, "What do you find in Ting-chou's teaching? Is there anything different from what you find here?"

The monk said, "Nothing different."

Wu-chiu said, "If there is nothing different, why don't you go back there?" and he hit him with his stick.

The monk said, "If your stick had eyes to see, you would not strike me like that."

Wu-chiu said, "Today I have come across a monk," and he gave him three more blows.

The monk went out. Wu-chiu called after him and

said, "One may receive unfair blows."

The monk turned back and said, "To my regret the stick is in your hand."

Wu-chiu said, "If you need it I will let you have it."

The monk went up to Wu-chiu, seized his stick, and gave him three blows with it.

Wu-chiu said, "Unfair blows! Unfair blows!"

The monk said, "One may receive them."

Wu-chiu said, "I hit this one too casually."

The monk made bows.

Wu-chiu said, "Monk! Is that how you take leave?"

The monk laughed aloud and went out.

Wu-chiu said, "That's it! That's it!"

The usual conceptual mode of thinking is upset by the apparently unsatisfying advice given in the koans by Zen masters to their disciples—the logical mind has nothing to reason with. Even in our explanation of how koans function, we essentially defeat their entire purpose. In the koan practice, we see how Zen desires to lessen our reliance on concepts, to shatter the rigid thought forms through which we seek to possess life; and in order to do so it makes devastating use of contradiction and paradox. Zen also possesses a total denial of opposites: it exposes the truth by using neither assertion nor negation. Ummon says, "In Zen there is absolute freedom: sometimes it negates and sometimes it affirms; it does either way at pleasure." Zen, in short, denies all attempts to rationalize it, make sense of it, or turn it into a philosophy. It compares man's desire to grasp it intellectually to a finger pointing to the moon–the finger

Above: Black iron mask with silver eyes.
Right: A wood and ivory statuette of a kneeling fox priest.

continually being mistaken for the moon itself. One should not bite at the finger of the Zen master, but look at where it is pointing. In a sense, the Western attempt to delineate and define everything has led to the exact opposite of Zen. In reading this book and absorbing its content you have two choices: either to take the material into your everyday rational existence, or alternatively, allow it to pass by and feel the gentle wind it creates. The more one tries to absorb and understand Zen, the more it escapes one. It is like grasping the cord of a veil and pulling it over your eyes; the very act of understanding blinds you to the essence.

In our everyday lives in Western society, this acceptance of Zen is of the greatest importance if we wish to experience its teachings, for we are conditioned to fail from the outset. And yet to find Zen in the "civilized" world is to discover something utterly unique and incomprehensible–like the sound of one hand clapping.

BIBLIOGRAPHY

Blyth, R.H., *Zen in English Literature and Oriental Classics,* Hokuseido, Tokyo, 1948

Dumoulin, Heinrich, *Zen Enlightenment — Origins and Meaning,* Weatherhill, New York and Tokyo, 1989

Humphreys, C., *Zen Buddhism,* Heinemann, London, 1949; Unwin Hyman, 1988

Osho, *Zen: The Quantum Leap from Mind to No-Mind,* Rebel Publishing House GmbH, Cologne, 1988

This. This. A Thousand Times This., Rebel Publishing House GmbH, Cologne, 1988

Watts, Alan W., *The Way of Zen,* Random House, New York, 1965

Faure, Bernard, *The Rhetoric of Immediacy: A Cultural Critique of Chan/Zen Buddhism,* Princeton University Press, Princeton, New Jersey, 1991

Kraft, Kenneth, ed., *Zen: Tradition and Transformation. A Sourcebook by Contemporary Zen Masters and Scholars,* Grove Weidenfeld, New York, 1988

Miura, Isshin and Ruth Sasaki, *Zen Dust,* Harcourt, Brace and World, Inc., New York, 1966

Suzuki, DaiseteT. *An Introduction to Zen Buddhism,* Grove Weidenfeld, New York, 1987

Yampolsky, Philip B., *The Platform Sutra of the Sixth Patriarch,* Columbia University Press, New York, 1967, 1978 (paperback)

ACKNOWLEDGMENTS

While every effort has been made to trace all present copyright holders of the material in this book, whether companies or individuals, any unintentional omission is hereby apologized for in advance and we will be pleased to correct any errors in acknowledgments in any future edition of this book.

Text acknowledgments:

pp. 14-16 — From Osho, *Zen: The Quantum Leap from Mind to No-Mind*, Rebel Publishing House GmbH, Cologne, 1988. Reproduced by permission of the publisher.

p. 30, and 34 — From Heinrich Dumoulin, *Zen Enlightenment — Origins and Meaning*, Weatherhill, New York and Tokyo, 1989. Reproduced by permission of the publisher.

p. 38 — From Alan W. Watts, *The Way of Zen*, Arkana Penguin Books, London, 1990. Reproduced by permission of the copyright holder, Thames & Hudson, London.

p. 52 — From Osho, *This. This. A Thousand Times This.*, Rebel Publishing House GmbH, Cologne, 1988. Reproduced by permission of the publisher.

pp. 54-55 — From Osho, *This. This. A Thousand Times This.*, Rebel Publishing House GmbH, Cologne, 1988. Reproduced by permission of the publisher.

Picture acknowledgments:

Courtesy of the Trustees of the Victoria & Albert Museum; Pages: 10, 17, 29, 52, 53, 56.
Christies Images; Pages: 4, 7, 16, 21, 24, 32, 33, 35, 39, 40, 41, 43, 49, 51, 54, 55, 57.
Camera Press, London; Pages: 8, 9.
Ancient Art and Architecture Collection, London; Pages: 36, 37, 58.
Copyright British Museum; Pages: 15, 26, 31, 46, 47, 48.
Hugh O'Donnell; Pages: 18, 19, 50.
Sosei Kuzunishi; Pages: 23, 25, 44, 45, 49.